# ABORIGINAL
# *Dreamtime*
# JOURNAL

## BY MEL BROWN, NGUNNAWAL WOMAN

ROCKPOOL

# DREAMTIME

Dreamtime relates to the stories that encompass our Aboriginal values, beliefs and lore – essentially Dreamtime is the ancient wisdom of the Ancestors that is passed down through our stories of creation. Our creation stories depict our values and the ways to live our lives while being at one with Mother Earth and Father Sun.

# Dear reader

In my Dreaming ... Mother Earth quietly whispers of ancient stories and shares her wisdom, so that we can be enlightened to better understand the purpose of our own journey of Dreaming.

In my Dreaming ... the Ancestors share knowledge and wisdom in the hope it is used wisely to create better outcomes for those who are open to listening to what the wise ones have to share.

Our Dreaming journey includes the many paths we take and choices we make during our human existence, including initiation, ceremony, rites of passage and the many phases of life we move through till eventually we return to Mother Earth.

Our ever-changing Dreaming allows our past to teach us how to live our lives in the present, so that our future is determined by the learning we experience today.

Aboriginal Dreaming encompasses our past, present and future. Our Dreaming is fluid and changes with each breath we take, each step we take and with each dream we dare to follow.

My hope is that this journal offers a chance for you to better understand your Dreaming, so that you can navigate your consciousness towards empowerment and self-healing.

With love,

Mel

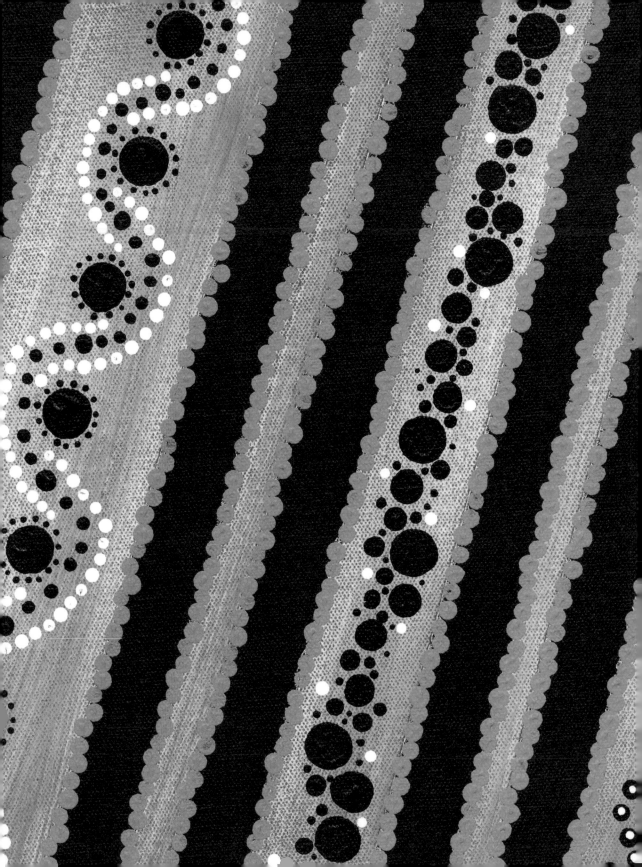

# HOW TO USE YOUR DREAMTIME JOURNAL

The *Aboriginal Dreamtime Journal* is a tool to give meaning and understanding to the past, assist us to identify ways in which to move forward in the present and, finally, draw upon our wisdom to illuminate our future Dreaming.

**Your Dreamtime Journal is divided into three sections:**

## PAST – record your memories of the past

Consider the past as your Dreamtime, where your stories of self-creation shaped you into who you are today. Looking back in reflection, record your thoughts in hindsight as a means of understanding how the past leads us towards the next steps we take in our future.

## PRESENT – record daily thoughts and events as they occur

Clarify your thoughts about the things that are happening now. Test their reality and the possibilities that lay ahead as you choose your next steps. Consider today's decisions as a means of preparing for your next decisions that lead you to your future.

## FUTURE – record your hopes and wishes for the future

By planning your future you begin to create what you want it to be. Surround yourself with your dreams as your future is limitless and nothing is too much to wish and hope for. What do you want your future to look like?

A selection of artwork taken from the author's previously published *Aboriginal Oracle Cards* was chosen for each section of the *Aboriginal Dreamtime Journal* to inspire and provoke thought and insight.

Each piece of artwork relates to either the past, present or future to assist you to examine your past, live in the present and dream of the future.

# PAST

Our Ancestors have lived lives prior to our existence and can see the future before us. It is within this knowledge that the Ancestors shed light on the darkness that can sometimes envelop our souls and leave us questioning the future.

Our Ancestors teach us to be strong and to explore the meaning of the moments that change our lives; they can also help us to find the determination for life to be different.

Write about events and times that represent your Past Dreaming – those moments in life where your thoughts or actions have resulted in meaningful transformation from who you were to who you are now.

Use the prompts on the following pages to record those precious moments when the voice in your head spoke words of wisdom – those words that changed your life – whether it was just a recognition of something you already knew but refused to acknowledge or a time when you found the courage to take your next step.

# FAITH

Loving and then letting go is not only one of the most challenging things we can do, it's also the bravest. Take big deep breaths and leave the past behind.

# LOVE

Before you can truly love another you need to open your heart and allow yourself to receive it first. If you open your heart to love it will flow into your very soul.

# WORTHWHILE

Life is not about being taught a lesson for getting something wrong – it's to have an experience that adds richness to our lives.

# CREATION

Creation is all around us, yet we never stop to appreciate it. Creation is as simple as a new idea you recognise as being something important to you. Give your idea life, and it will become one of those moments in time when you remember what a fantastic idea it was.

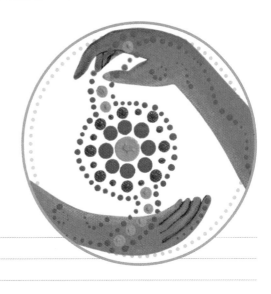

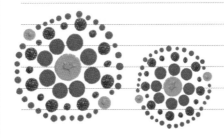

# HIDDEN LEARNING

Letting go of what you hold close is really hard sometimes, but often it's because you can't let go that the most damage is caused.

Take a leap of faith and know that by letting go you are actually allowing growth.

Each person's journey is individual and we have little power over what is best for them.

# SEASONS CHANGE

As we grow our relationships change, and we need to adapt to the change or risk being left behind or even losing them.

It's not always easy, but if change is what is needed then consider the challenge as an investment in your future.

# SPIRITUAL AWAKENING

Have you ever experienced that light-bulb moment when suddenly everything just fits in place? Where the key pieces of the puzzle finally fit and things begin to take shape?

Spiritual awakening is a profound moment in time, and embraces a true sense of understanding from your very soul.

Revelations bring you closer to 'self' and provide you with a foundation on which to understand yourself at a far deeper and more spiritual level than you have before.

There may still be some ways to go, however, this is the beginning of a new journey in your life story.

# MAGICKAL DREAMING

Dreaming is the path on which we travel during our journey in this and past lifetimes. Often our Dreaming may follow a similar track lifetime after lifetime, in different bodies and different countries, but still covering familiar territory.

Finding the courage to traverse paths less travelled is what our Dreaming is really about. Allowing the soul to have different experiences is the way in which we grow emotionally and spiritually.

# ANCESTRAL HEALING

Ancestral healing is twofold: it is the healing of the soul throughout the lifetimes we live, and it is calling on the wisdom of our Elders who have passed before us to guide us on our journey.

Our soul has suffered many traumas and brings forth these hurts into our present lifetime as cellular memory – causing us to act and react in certain ways with no concept as to why.

Healing our spirit is the journey that brings us to connect to spirit and form relationships with our Ancestors.

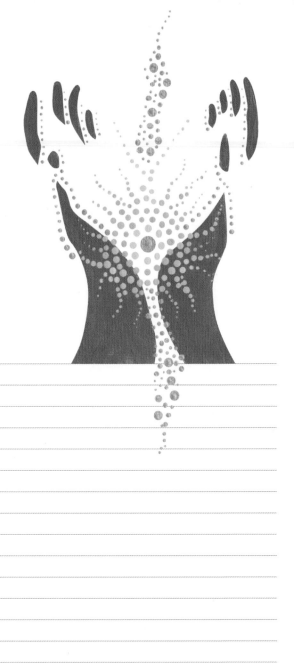

# SPIRITUAL ASCENSION

There is no magick formula for finding the path that best suits your spiritual growth, and for each of us it is an individual journey that becomes our story.

We create our own Dreaming by walking our own tracks and learning from our own experiences.

Sometimes we can walk together with others down the exact same track and experience the exact same thing, however, what we learn from our journey can be entirely different and unique for each of us.

# HONESTY

In your search for honesty, first look within.

# WISDOM

Wisdom is born of those who have passed before us and are open to sharing their knowledge. This transfer of knowledge can only be attained if you spend time in conversation with the Ancestors.

Stop and listen and benefit from the wisdom that is available to be shared with you.

# SYDNEY THE FRILL-NECKED LIZARD

Sydney the Frill-necked Lizard pretends to be
brave even when she is frightened and wants
to run away.

# STANLEY THE RED-BELLIED BLACK SNAKE

Stanley the Red-bellied Black Snake sheds
his skin so that each year he can grow
bigger and wiser.

# ANCESTRAL WISDOM

Ancestral Wisdom is cellular memory stored in your body, bringing forth memories from times long ago.

Ancestral Wisdom remembers your past-life experiences and hopes you trust this information with blind faith.

Ancestral Wisdom is passed from generation to generation and from one life to the next. Learn to recognise this and begin to trust in yourself and allow this instinctual knowledge to flow freely.

Learn to work with your intuitive energies and trust the messages and feelings that come so easily to you.

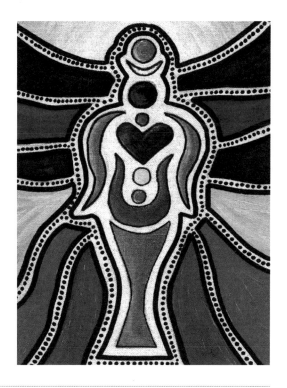

---
---
---
---
---
---
---
---
---
---
---

# FATHER SKY

Father Sky is the spirit of the night and the day, the moon, the stars and the sun. He represents All that is above the ground, out into the endless universe and beyond.

    Father Sky is the seer of dark and light, good and bad, yet with his eternal wisdom he does not judge.

# MOTHER GODDESS

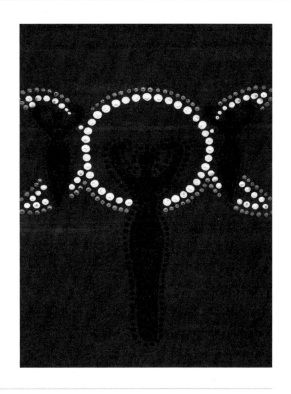

Mother Goddess is known by many names, yet she stands above all. We are all born from her womb.

Mother Goddess is the keeper of wisdom and truth, and has the ability to create what she deems as necessary. She is our true Mother and works only from a place of true unconditional love. She just simply IS.

Mother Goddess is not limited by time and space – she can see beyond today and tomorrow and look back into the past. You have the ability to see into the future and create what you need.

# REFLECTION

Reflection is the ability to look back and see a situation for what it was. It's those moments when you may see things in a different light once you have been given the gift of clarity.

Reflection is often referred to as hindsight, but the key to insight is what you do with the information once you have discovered it. Your choice is to either learn from it or continue on as before.

Reflection is our quiet time when we have the opportunity to reassess and make changes in our lives or acknowledge the journey on which we have embarked.

# RETURN TO COUNTRY

Returning to Country is when Aboriginal People return to where they were born, and where their family's spiritual links are.

It's a spiritual journey returning our people to their Dreaming, and a time to explore and challenge your history, reclaim who you are and redefine your identity.

Sometimes we can change our outlook on life by looking back, seeing things for what they were and valuing the lessons and wisdom learned as a result of our experiences. It's time to let go of the past and embrace the future.

# PRESENT

Our Ancestors watch over us throughout our Dreaming and are always sharing knowledge and wisdom, by coincidences that occur, random words from a friend or stranger, a whisper to your subconscious or a message in your dreams, providing you with insight and sometimes the courage to take the next step on your journey.

Our Present Dreaming is made up of many paths and many choices, all of which lead in certain directions and write our history. With the exhale of each breath we write our Past Dreaming, and with our next breath we step into our Present Dreaming, always moving towards our Future Dreaming.

Each step we take, every decision we make and each experience we have in the 'now' represents our Present Dreaming. Our 'here and now' shapes the decisions we make and the future paths we take on our life's journey.

In this section of the journal, use the prompts on the following pages to record your experiences and thoughts that are occurring now and how they impact on your life.

# AMAZEMENT

You have worked hard to get everything just the way it is right now. Trust and enjoy this moment – everything is as it should be.

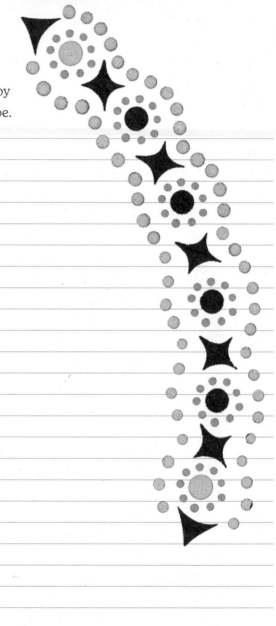

# CALM

Breathe ... heal your tired body and allow your spirit to find its peace. Without harmony your healing journey will take so much longer.

# CONFIDENCE

Just believe in magick. You don't need an
explanation for everything – trust it has
happened for all the right reasons.

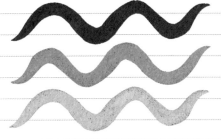

# SELF-LOVE

Self-love is not egotistical. It shows yourself
and others that you are worthwhile and
deserve love in all its many forms.

# MOON PHASES

Our Dreaming journey takes us on many different paths, within many different cycles. The waxing and waning of the moon is just one of those cycles.

In life there are highs and lows, but somehow our lives find balance. Look to the cycles in your life to get a better understanding of what your journey should look like, learn from the lows and celebrate the highs and then find the middle ground.

# PEACE

Take time out to find the peace that is so elusive. The harder we try to make time for peace in our life the further away it gets.

Wait till everything lines up, take a breath and in that breath find the peace that is within the very breath itself. Breathe through difficult times, still your mind and peace will find you.

# QUIET STILLNESS

Change is not a bad thing. Weigh up all the pros and cons and find the courage to make a commitment – one way or the other.

You can always return to the way it was before, but it may be nice to experience something different for a while.

# TWILIGHT SHADOWS

Often we concentrate our energy on what
we can't have or can't achieve, and this is
when our self-esteem begins to deteriorate
and issues start to weigh us down.

Forget the problem and look at what
you are able to do and are capable of, then
work from there. There are times when our
problems are only about our inability to
see the strengths we possess.

# LADY OF THE LAKE

It is important to value your beliefs – they are what have guided you in your life's journey.

Often we are tempted by other ideas that seem more glamorous or hold a promise of greater riches; however, when making such life-changing decisions take a moment to check your real feelings.

# ANCIENT KNOWLEDGE

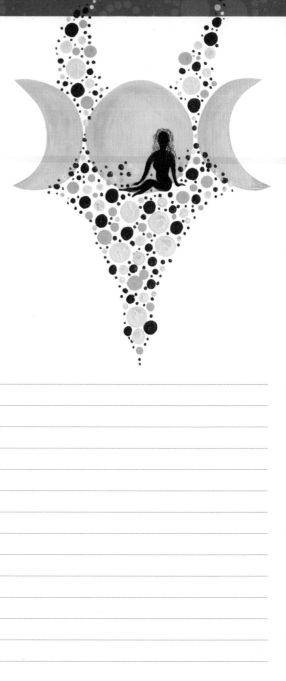

We need to allow ourselves to trust our wisdom and cease searching for evidence to back up our thoughts and feelings.

We each possess knowledge that is unique, as no one else can walk in your shoes and know your stories.

Everything we need to know can be found within, so trust in yourself and your own wisdom. Wisdom is never lost, just buried under piles of self-doubt.

Remember what it is like to have the courage to stand in your own power and make your own decisions.

# DIVINE MESSENGER

Listen to the inner voices in your head – this is where you will find the wisdom you seek.

   Often we do not hear the answers because they are not the answers we want to hear.

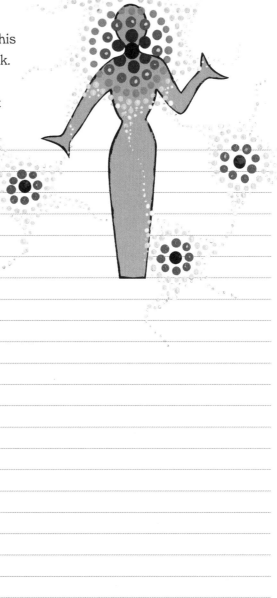

# GREEN CHAKRA GODDESS

Go outside and touch the ground, and take a few deep breaths to reconnect to the vitality Mother Earth has to offer.

Allow the energies of Mother Earth to recharge your batteries as she shares herself with you. You will be amazed at how quickly you feel refreshed and recharged by taking these simple steps.

This is a gentle reminder of how important your connection to nature is and how easy it is to find strength from Mother Earth.

# ACCEPTANCE

Acceptance is a humbling experience and a difficult emotion to nurture and develop.

Acceptance means trusting that everything is exactly where it is supposed to be. When life throws at you its best and worst, acceptance is trusting it is all part of the journey.

Recognising and finding the tolerance and understanding we need to get through such situations is truly the stuff that spiritual accession is all about.

# SACRED LEARNING

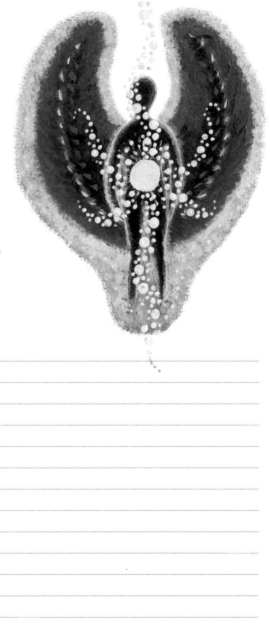

The origin of sacred learning begins at the birth of time. Some may say time is endless and there is no beginning and no end.

Our learning is not dissimilar – there is no beginning and no end. While ever there is breath in our being we are still learning.

Recognising your spiritual knowledge is a gift of memories you have stored over many lifetimes and experiences. Sacred learning comes from your ability to first recognise this knowledge and then believe in yourself to find the courage to integrate it into your life.

It is an internal knowing that guides us to where we need to be.

# RELEASE

Release can be challenging, as it can mean handing over control to another or to the universe. Trusting another source to provide for your needs and wants requires courage.

The other side of release is letting go of something simply through fear of what may happen if you stick it out. Fear of success, fear of failure, fear of the unknown. At times it is easier to let go than to see where a situation leads, particularly if you're experienced at managing loss.

# WHOLENESS OF SELF

Recapture your sense of adventure, have some fun and just be naughty.

It's time to experience life like everyone else and make mistakes just like them!

# UNIVERSAL UNDERSTANDING

The true power of universal understanding is in the palm of your hand. It will not be found in books or by seeking wisdom from others; it is found within yourself.

It is about trusting your instincts and knowing what your truth is – it may be different from others, but their experiences are different from yours.

# CHERRY BALLART

Cherry ballart medicine brings courage and hope to those who are optimistic.

Positivity is not always welcomed by others, particularly if they themselves are hurting.

When you express your hopefulness others may be too scared to feel the same way. While enthusiasm can be contagious, it can sometimes be destructive – particularly for those who are not in the same position and fearful of being hurt even more if the promises of 'sunshine and rainbows' don't come to fruition.

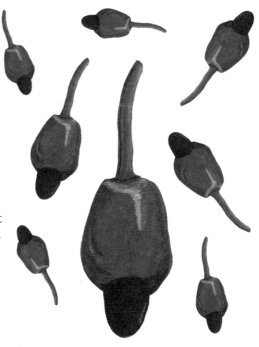

# KANGAROO PLUM

Kangaroo plum medicine is connected to truth and honesty.

Speaking one's own truth is a rare thing that takes courage and trust, not only for the speaker but also for the listener. However, there is a responsibility to speak your truth in a way that does not hurt or harm others.

When hiding behind the words 'I have a right to speak my truth', beware that you don't hurt others.

# SPINY-HEADED MAT-RUSH

Spiny-headed mat-rush medicine allows us to understand the complexity of a situation.

Sometimes we make things so difficult that managing a situation can become insurmountable. Don't allow this to be an excuse not to undertake the challenging work and search for the answers that might require you to change your behaviour or beliefs.

Change is not easy and means leaving old ways behind to adopt new ways, but change can bring healing and opportunity.

# CONTENTMENT

Contentment is appreciating that place within where serenity and happiness can be found.

# INTEGRITY

Integrity is the ability to allow others
to have their own experiences
without fear of judgement.

# JOSHUA THE TASMANIAN DEVIL

Joshua the Tasmanian devil is not afraid to take on a big challenge; just because he is small doesn't mean he is weak.

# KENNY COCKATOO

Kenny Cockatoo loves the freedom of
flying around and having adventures
with his mates.

# CONFUSION

Is the cup half full or half empty? What comes first: the chicken or the egg? Things that are logical can seem confusing.

The gut says one thing, the head says another, while the heart says something else again. In which do we trust? We trust in ourselves.

We trust in our values and morals. We try to keep our attitude positive and know confusion is only a temporary state that places doubts in our heads but also provides the opportunity to re-evaluate.

# FREEDOM

Your sense of freedom only comes from feeling content within yourself. Freedom is about being able to make decisions in your life without constraints holding you back.

We can all find our freedom in some form or another, from a walk in the bush to quieting our minds in a beautifully calming meditation. Freedom is within everyone's grasp, but first work out what your freedom is ...

# GROWTH

Growth is the cycle of life yet there are cycles within cycles, helping us grow a little at a time so as not to overwhelm us.

The end result is defined as an achievement, however, often during the growth cycle events will occur that can challenge and stunt our growth.

The same is to be said of a sapling growing into a mature tree. Over its lifetime the tree will experience challenges such as drought, flood and fire. This will stunt the tree's growth for a time till the conditions are right for growth again. Only then will the sapling have the opportunity to reach full maturity as a sturdy and bountiful tree brimming with life.

# INDECISIVE

There are many reasons why we lack courage to make hard decisions. During this limbo period we can be struck by fear, a sense of incompleteness. During this indecisive time we doubt ourselves.

We lose our self-confidence and look to others for guidance. It's ok to look to others for assistance, but ensure you trust your own intuition during these times.

Sometimes we just need to find that quiet space to listen to ourselves – the answers will always come.

# SADNESS

Sometimes in our lives we come to the fork in the path and find it difficult to decide on our next path.

If we procrastinate on the side of the road for too long the universe gives us a little shove to help us get moving again.

Sadness can be debilitating for someone who finds themselves in this dark place. It can also be a cleansing emotion, as it marks a point where you recognise circumstances may have to change to allow you to move forward on your journey.

# TRUTH

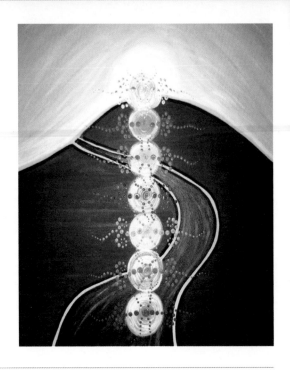

Truth is not just simply your own understanding of how things are, for truth is deeper than that. It is an unspoken knowing that comes from deep within. It is the soul acknowledging the truth in its purest form.

Truth can often be clouded by others' interpretations of life, yet your soul has a remarkable way of distinguishing what is real and what is not.

Spend time listening and taking note of your body as all the answers are there within – just look inside and listen.

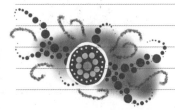

# FUTURE

The decisions previously made now begin to ripple into the future. Like a stone thrown into a still pond, these ripples begin to merge with others and change the surface of the pond.

Some moments will be tough while others will be wondrous, but if we keep our focus on the edge of the pond eventually we make it to the smooth water, where we can savour the peace we have found.

The future is what you make it. Every thought and action you take today creates tomorrow. Tomorrow can be full of hope, love and laughter ... what are you creating? Live the life you want your great grandchildren to have ... because it starts with you.

Use the prompts on the following pages to record your best future. Be brave and imagine a life where your dreams become your reality, surrounded by people who share in your new life. Nothing is too impossible to dream into being.

# RICHNESS

Search further. The deeper you explore an issue the more truth you will find – it will be well worth the effort.

# SUCCESS

You are worthy of this success. Allow these
feelings of accomplishment to fill you with
contentment and the self-satisfaction of
your achievement.

# WONDERFUL

Sometimes being too cautious is just an excuse for being afraid to take risks and move forward. Don't use this as your excuse to miss out on something amazing!

# DREAMING

Dreams can provide you with the answers
you're looking for. Begin to take notice of
your dreams as they are often prophetic.

# INSIGHTFUL REVELATIONS

Our heads are full of ideas, but it's the idea within the idea that gives us the most satisfaction – you know, the idea that grows from a singular thought into a reality and looks nothing like the original idea but is better than that first idea?

Consider your ideas as having the potential to create amazing changes in your life.

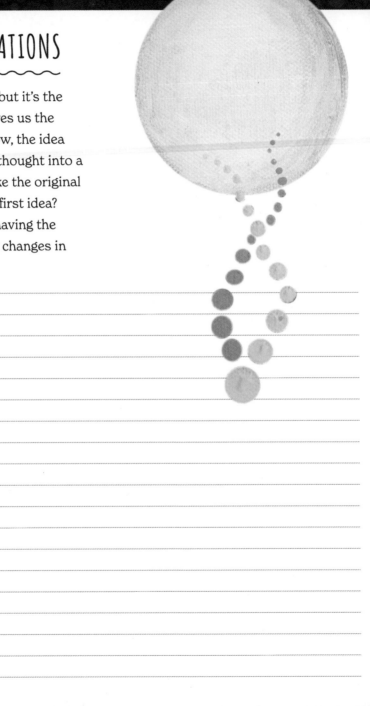

# REBIRTH

It's time to stretch your wings. You like the comfort of what you know and change can be a challenge for you, but sometimes it can be used as an excuse to never take a chance.

It's time to leave the comfort of your nest and make a move. The benefits of the change can outweigh the challenges, so just make the move!

# SACRED BEGINNINGS

Everything starts small, and to move forward takes incredible courage.

The search for courage is the hardest part of any journey but, in turn, is the ultimate achievement.

From courage you gain confidence; whether it's the confidence to just give it a go ... you're already a winner. Take a deep breath and just move forward.

# WONDROUS OPPORTUNITIES

Working on your own gives you confidence to create unique opportunities that can be highly beneficial to you.

However, in your quest to work alone you can miss out on the creativity and relationships that occur when you work with others.

Seek the company of others, as there is a lot to be gained from sharing information and skills.

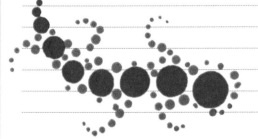

# BUDDHA

Your inner wisdom provides you with a glimpse of the world and opportunities beyond this situation.

Be brave and step away; seek the greater knowledge that is within your reach, and as a result of such efforts changes will inevitably occur.

# COURAGEOUS INTENT

Courage is not limited to bold and daring acts – in fact, the most elusive courage to find is that which lays within your very self.

It's the ability to dig deep and not only find but then listen to your own inner wisdom. The next step is to trust your wisdom and act accordingly. This is the true test of blind faith and is what courageous intent is really about.

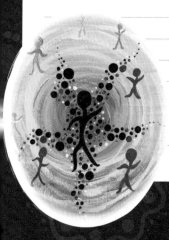

# FERTILITY

Fertility is about birth and growth. It is about having the courage to seek new opportunities and the wisdom to grow from these experiences.

   The beauty of new experiences is they provide opportunities to create outcomes that could not be manifested without the chance to grow.

   Watching dreams and wishes grow and develop in front of your own eyes is a truly spiritual journey – a journey filled with wonderful stories awaiting the right circumstances to blossom into fairy tales.

# CHICKWEED

Chickweed medicine encourages you to develop and grow.

Growing does not occur without change, yet change can sometimes be unimaginable. For some the power of knowing what to expect and how to control it provides a sense of security, which has become a survival technique.

What is taken away must be replaced, or else cracks begin to occur and holes begin to form. Sometimes the cracks simply fill with water and provide an opportunity for new growth to begin.

# FARMER'S FRIEND

Farmer's friend medicine allows us to see through the exaggerated views of others.

When we experience things that touch on past unresolved emotions our reactions can become exaggerated.

It is empowering to understand where these emotions might be coming from to better understand how they affect us and those around us.

# ECHIDNA

Echidna waddles at a slow pace yet is determined to reach his destination, never distracted or straying from his purpose. If obstacles appear on his route he simply improvises, changes direction and goes around them.

Echidna's ability to carry on regardless of what is happening around him demonstrates his skill in staying focused and attaining his goal of completing the task.

# EMU

Emu is the most inquisitive of creatures and an eternal optimist, always searching for situations that he can turn into opportunities.

Possessing a boldness that provides him with the courage to take chances and go places he has yet to explore, Emu is not afraid to seek out further knowledge.

His offspring quickly learn that seeking new experiences is not to be feared but embraced and the journey itself is part of the knowledge they will gain. While in Emu's own travels, he will open himself to boundless opportunities.

# BEATRICE THE CUTTLEFISH

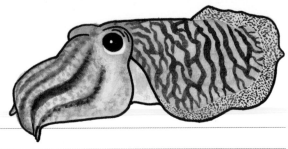

Beatrice the Cuttlefish is good at fitting into new surroundings and is fearless when beginning new adventures.

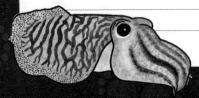

# CODY THE KOALA

Cody the Koala never hurries and takes his time to achieve his goals.

# INNER HARMONY

Our inner harmony can only flow when we are true to ourselves and walk our own path. Inner harmony is made up of many emotions; however, take all of this away and you are left with 'you'.

Inner harmony is a place of quiet stillness where you know and love yourself for who you are.

It is a place of great respect for the journey you are on and of the experience that is gifted to you. It's the recognition of the spirit within yourself that gives you your ultimate connection to 'self'.

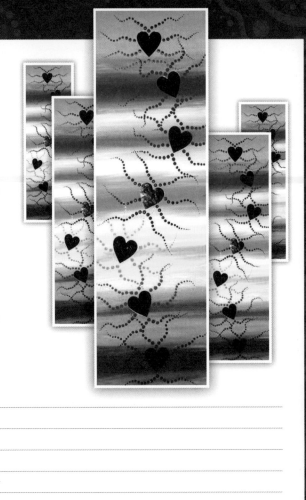

# MANIFESTATION

Manifestation is just a new name for principles that have been practised for thousands of years and used across many realms. Whether it is praying to the gods for a good harvest or making a totem for good luck or protection it's all the same thing. It's about creating an outcome that you desire.

Whether manifesting is created by ceremony or ritual or by putting the thought out to the universe, it's simply a different path to the same destination – and a different name for an ancient practice.

# RESPONSIBILITY

Responsibility is ultimately defined as taking control of your own journey. It is knowing what your role is and then taking steps to live that life.

Responsibility is not about blaming others or holding them accountable but acknowledging what your part was in the situation and learning from the experience.

# MATILDA THE BOGONG MOTH

Matilda the Bogong Moth constantly
amazes her friends with her ability to
see the beauty in each day.

# CREATIVITY

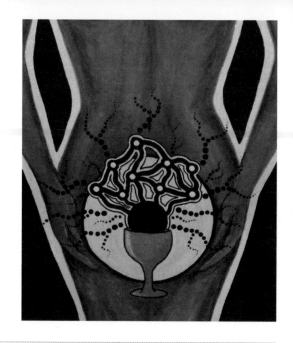

Creativity has been with us since the dawning of time. It is our very essence. It is life itself. It is Creation.

Creativity gives us each the freedom of expression to be who we truly are and the opportunity to create what is meaningful and important for ourselves.

Creative vision is only limited by imagination and inspiration. What inspires each of us is uniquely individual and should be honoured and respected by our own self.

# ABOUT THE AUTHOR

**Melinda Brown is a Ngunnawal woman who resides in the Northern Rivers Bundjalung Nation and has attained a Master's in Indigenous Healing and Trauma.**

Mel embraced her clairvoyant skills many years ago, and embarked on a journey to understand that her spiritual beliefs were not just limited to her Aboriginal culture but encompassed many different types of beliefs from across the world.

Mel has a unique way of highlighting that the ownership of spirituality belongs to each individual and is not defined by labels or limited to just one understanding of life and creation, and as human beings our spiritual needs cannot usually be met by one singular belief system.

The melding of cultures and spiritual beliefs led Mel to create a range of Aboriginal oracle cards that are being increasingly recognised across the world. She is always working on the next deck, and embraces her creativity as a therapeutic way to better understand that spirituality is unique and individual for all our brothers and sisters across the universe.

As a professional speaker and trainer, Mel is known for her expertise in Aboriginal cultural competency and lateral violence both nationally and internationally.

**spiritdreaming.com.au**